# THE CANTICLE OF THE CREATURES

*for Saint Francis of Assisi*

# THE CANTICLE OF THE CREATURES

## for Saint Francis of Assisi

Luigi Santucci

Translated by Demetrio S. Yocum
Illustrated by Br. Martin Erspamer, OSB

PARACLETE PRESS
BREWSTER, MASSACHUSETTS

2017 First printing

*The Canticle of the Creatures for Saint Francis of Assisi*

English translation copyright © 2017 by Demetrio S. Yocum
Illustrations copyright © 2017 by Martin Erspamer, OSB

ISBN 978-1-61261-775-6

Originally published in Italian as *La lode degli animali* (Edizioni Messaggero Padova, 1981).

Excerpts labeled FAED are from Francis of Assisi: Early Documents, volumes 1–3, ed. Regis J. Armstrong, OFM, J. A. Wayne Hellmann, OFM, William J. Short, OFM (New York: New City Press, 1999–2002), used by permission of the publisher.

Scripture references are taken from the New Revised Standard Version Bible, copyright © 1989 by the Division of Education of the National Council of Churches of Christ in the U.S.A., and are used by permission. All rights reserved.

The Paraclete Press name and logo (dove on cross) are trademarks of Paraclete Press, Inc.

Library of Congress Cataloging-in-Publication Data:
Names: Santucci, Luigi, author. | Erspamer, Martin, 1953- illustrator.
Title: The canticle of the creatures : for Saint Francis of Assisi / Luigi
  Santucci ; translated by Demetrio S. Yocum ; illustrations by Martin
  Erspamer, OSB.
Other titles: Lode degli animali. English
Description: Brewster, Massachusetts : Paraclete Press Inc., 2017. | Includes
  bibliographical references and index.
Identifiers: LCCN 2017022180 | ISBN 9781612617756 (hardcover : alk. paper) Subjects:
LCSH: Francis, of Assisi, Saint, 1182-1226--Fiction.Classification: LCC PQ4841.A67
L6313 2017 | DDC 853/.914--dc23LC record available at https://lccn.loc.gov/2017022180

10 9 8 7 6 5 4 3 2 1

Published by Paraclete Press
Brewster, Massachusetts
www.paracletepress.com

Printed in the United States of America

*It came to pass*

*by a supernatural influx of power*

*that the nature of brute animals*

*was moved in some gracious manner*

*toward him.*

—ST. BONAVENTURE

Heaven and earth glorify God. All the creatures proclaim his existence. The heaven cries to God: "You it was who made me: I did not make myself." And the earth cries: "You are my creator: you it was who made me."

But when and how do they proclaim this truth? When humankind reflects on them and on this truth, therein precisely is the answer. It is thanks to your careful examination of them, it is thanks to your voice that they have a voice.

Look at the heavens: how beautiful they are! And look at the earth: how beautiful it is! Both heaven and earth radiate beauty.

God has made them, he directs them, he orders their course, is always present in their history, he determines their importance and arranges them in relation to his nature. That is why all creatures glorify him, those that move and those that are static, the heavens above and the earth below, perennial youth and august old age.

*This spectacle which has been given you to admire, the joy with which it inspires you, the impetus with which it raises you up to the Maker of it all, the revelation of the ineffable Being through whom he created it—all this is the testimony of heaven and earth to which you bear witness when you look at them.*

*Because he has made every object, because no object is greater than he, all his works are as it were within him, as though contained in him. If you love what he has made, love still more him who has made it all. If the creation is beautiful, God who is reflected in it is infinitely more beautiful.*[1]

—ST. AUGUSTINE

hrough the love of the most sublime poverty, the man of God prospered and grew rich in holy simplicity. Although he certainly possessed nothing of his own in this world, he seemed to possess all good things in the very Author of this world. With the steady gaze of a dove, that is, the simple application and pure consideration of the mind, he referred all things to the supreme Artisan and recognized, loved, and praised their Maker in all things. It came to pass, by a heavenly gift of kindness, that he possessed all things in God and God in all things. In consideration of the primal origin of all things, he would call all creatures, however insignificant, by the names of brother and sister since they come forth with him from the one source. He embraced those, however, more tenderly and passionately, who portray by a natural likeness the gracious gentleness of Christ and exemplify it in the Scriptures. It came to pass by a supernatural influx of power that the nature of brute animals was moved in some gracious manner toward him. Even inanimate things obeyed his command, as if this same holy man, so simple and upright, had already returned to the state of innocence.[2]

— ST. BONAVENTURE

# CONTENTS

# ON SAINT FRANCIS OF ASSISI

—BY POPE FRANCIS

BELIEVE THAT SAINT FRANCIS IS the example par excellence of care for the vulnerable and of an integral ecology lived out joyfully and authentically. He is the patron saint of all who study and work in the area of ecology, and he is also much loved by non-Christians. He was particularly concerned for God's creation and for the poor and outcast. He loved, and was deeply loved for his joy, his generous self-giving, his openheartedness. He was a mystic and a pilgrim who lived in simplicity and in wonderful harmony with God, with others, with nature and with himself. He shows us just how inseparable the bond is between concern for nature, justice for the poor, commitment to society, and interior peace.

Francis helps us to see that an integral ecology calls for openness to categories which transcend the language of mathematics and biology, and take us to the heart of what it is to be human. Just as happens when we fall in love with someone, whenever he would gaze at the sun, the moon or the smallest of animals, he burst into song, drawing all other creatures into his praise. He communed with all creation, even preaching to the flowers, inviting them "to praise the Lord, just as if they were endowed with reason." His response to the world around him was so much more than intellectual appreciation or economic calculus, for to him each and every creature was a sister united to him by bonds of affection. That is why he felt called to care for all that exists. His disciple Saint Bonaventure tells us that, "from a reflection on the primary source of all things, filled with even more abundant piety, he would call creatures, no matter how small, by the name of 'brother' or 'sister'." Such a conviction cannot be written off as naive romanticism, for it affects the choices which determine our behaviour. If we approach nature and the environment without this openness to awe and wonder, if we no longer speak the language of fraternity and beauty in our relationship with the world, our attitude will be that of masters, consumers, ruthless exploiters, unable to set limits on their immediate needs. By contrast, if we feel intimately united with all that exists, then sobriety and care will well up spontaneously. The poverty and austerity of Saint Francis were no mere veneer of asceticism, but something much more radical: a refusal to turn reality into an object simply to be used and controlled.

What is more, Saint Francis, faithful to Scripture, invites us to see nature as a magnificent book in which God speaks to us and grants us a glimpse of his infinite beauty and goodness. "Through the greatness and the beauty of creatures one comes to know by analogy their maker" (Wisdom 13:5); indeed, "his eternal power and divinity have been made known through his works since the creation of the world" (Rom 1:20). For this reason, Francis asked that part of the friary garden always be left untouched, so that wild flowers and herbs could grow there, and those who saw them could raise their minds to God, the Creator of such beauty. Rather than a problem to be solved, the world is a joyful mystery to be contemplated with gladness and praise.[3]

# FOREWORD

S T. FRANCIS OF ASSISI'S MOST FAMOUS AND evocative sermons—between history and legend—that have come down to us are undoubtedly the sermons to the birds and the wolf of Gubbio. They reveal the most fascinating aspects and the deepest and most joyful gifts of the saint of Assisi, while offering at the same time a human and evangelical portrait of the man who has been called "the brother of all people and creatures."

The preaching to the birds was immortalized by Giotto in one of the most sublime paintings of all time, in the Upper Basilica of Assisi, in the first fresco on the left of those entering the basilica. As soon as you enter and stop to admire the fresco, you immediately feel you are on the threshold of the finally found "earthly paradise." In Giotto's fresco, Francis is talking to the birds, with serene and firm sweetness, and they listen to him attentively. . . . But who is really speaking, Francis or the birds?

I must confess that every time I find myself in front of that wonderful scene, so pure yet so full of mystery, I am tempted, better yet I hope, once I close my eyes, to be able to reverse that dialogue of the holy saint with his feathered listeners.

Is this fantasy of mine unwarranted, arbitrary, and heretical? Is it possible that the birds not only listened to Francis, but at times spoke to him? And if that is the case, as I am convinced, how can we not admit that animals have a soul in their own way?

In this book by Luigi Santucci, full of poetry, imagination, and joy, such a belief, which is not only mine, gains strength and conviction. Luigi Santucci, a master storyteller who in all his works has been able to reveal the dream within reality and the reality within the dream, by narrating the stories of the animals who appear in Francis's life, also endorses the notion that these animals have a soul and thus immortality. Such an opinion has mysterious and ancient origins. Some trace it back to St. Paul's famous remark that "creation waits with eager longing for the revealing of the children of God" (Romans 8:19), and to his other statement in which Christ is "the image of the invisible God, the firstborn of all creation" (Colossians 1:15), and thus not just of "man." Still others trace it further back, to the book of Ecclesiastes, where it is written: "For the fate of humans and the fate of animals is the same; as one dies, so dies the other. They all have the same breath, and humans have no advantage over the animals" (Ecclesiastes 3:19). And we know that intellectuals such as Johannes Scotus Eriugena, Lorenzo Valla, and Paracelsus openly professed that same belief (or opinion, or eccentricity). And, if we want to turn to more contemporary figures, even Paul VI once said in one of his audiences that "Animals are the smallest part of God's creation, but one day we will see them again in Christ's mystery."

Supported by these and other authoritative voices, I think I understand why Francis loved to listen more than to talk and preach. Like no one else after the first apostles, Francis was filled and driven by the Word of God; Thomas of Celano describes him as one who "made his whole body a tongue" (*de toto corpore fecerat linguam*). True, Francis was a unique itinerant evangelist, a popular preacher full of passion and simplicity; but, first, he was a humble, docile listener. Francis listened to all: the Holy Spirit and the leper, the wolf and the pope, the robbers and the lamb, the friars and the birds. He was able to discern the inaudible moan of the worm, even the almost imperceptible sound of tears furrowing a human face. That explains why he could be understood by both men and animals; and why, in the dialogue with both (perhaps, at times, with more abandon and joy in talking with the animals than with his fellow brothers), he was inspired by messages announcing penance, hope, and salvation to all. In his evangelism, Francis started the reconciliation between humans and animals, calling them all, with equal respect and love, "brothers," "sisters," and "friends," and by doing so, making them so. The episode of the Wolf of Gubbio, be it legend or symbol, exemplifies this practical teaching: cohabitation without suspicion and terror. For Francis, these innocent beings, dragged into "exile" with Adam and Eve, help us to find, in our hearts and in the created world, the path back to innocence and happiness.

We are familiar with the canticle that Francis sang and had others sing to God for all creatures; it is part of our poetry and our hope. However, only a few echoes and mentions emerging from Franciscan sources hint at what the animals sang for him. I am delighted—and I hope the readers will be too—that on this eighth centenary[4] of Francis's birth, a great storyteller like Luigi Santucci has dared, magnificently and successfully, to imagine in words a few lines of that song of praise, to help us give eyes and imagination to our faith, and faith to our imagination.

—FR. NAZARENO FABBRETTI

# THE CANTICLE OF THE CREATURES
*for Saint Francis of Assisi*

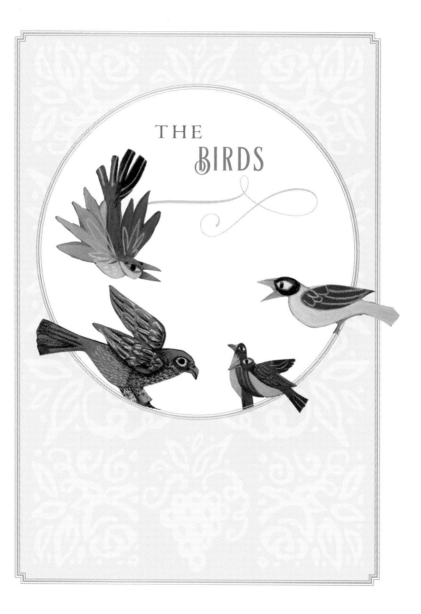

# THE
## BIRDS

# THE NIGHTINGALE

*In early morning at dawn, while he stood in prayer, birds of various kinds came over to the cell where he was staying. They did not come all together, but first one would come and sing its sweet verse, and then go away, and another one come and sing and go away. They all did the same. Blessed Francis was very happy at this and received great consolation from it.*[5]

THIS PRELUDE SONG IS FOR ME TO SING. For though all animals know how to communicate, or at least express themselves, I was given a gift of revelation that befits musicians and poets.

So we are the "animals"; or, if you like, the "beasts." But after meeting Francis, as it was granted to us, you can no longer say "brutes." The word "animal" is from *anima*, which means "soul," since we have souls. What is the soul? Something that "loves" and does not "die"; and does not die "precisely" "because it loves." Hence, neither will we die. Even if you keep killing us so easily, we will live forever.

Is not what we call "soul" this joy that makes me fly relentlessly in search of bugs and worms to satisfy the hunger of my little ones? And the joy with which your dog welcomes you after your return from a trip, whining and licking you all over, and the fear that keeps the hare crouching under the bush with its heart pounding to bursting, are not these part of what we call "soul"?

Like you, in some mysterious way, we will live forever; and the eternal paradise that awaits you we will share one day together. The fact remains that Francis would have loved us even if we were beings destined for a hopeless death—just because we came from the hands of the Creator: God's "creatures." But if that were the case, he would have loved us not with joy but with a deep sadness: the one with which the Hindu keep alive their animals and never eat their flesh; and when a cow lies down on the road, they prefer to stop their vehicles and wait rather than disturb her. And you must have heard the story of the prophet Muhammad, who, to avoid disturbing the cat sleeping curled on his sleeve while he was working, used his free hand to take scissors and sacrifice the hem of his robe. In the cases of benevolence by the followers of other faiths toward us animals, there is a fear of hurting us. While noble, these are not the same feelings Francis taught by revealing the cosmic heart of Christ in dealing with us. His message is a love for us full of fantasy, of eloquence, of extravagant games and subterfuge. His message is that you should approach us as when you were five or six years old—you would have woken up at dawn and walked for miles to fix the broken leg of a fledgling fallen from the nest, or to see a mythical creature, like a flying deer with iridescent wings.

But above all, Francis's message is about that feeling of compassion mentioned by St. Bonaventure, which does not mean just to avoid hurting us, or to help us; it means to recognize in your encounter with us the celestial moment of adoration. Charles Bonnet wrote that our souls, when compared to yours, are "in a state of infancy."[6] Perhaps, more simply, one can say that *we are* your childhood, and, as such, the best custodians of your most wonderful season in life.

Why did Francis love us this way and invite you to do the same? Why did he, in the many miraculous and touching episodes that the Franciscan sources handed down to you, invite you to see us as your brothers and sisters and to a certain extent, even as mentors? No doubt because we are colorful, lovely, and companionable. But also because we are, through our innocence, the mediators between you and the good Lord who has put us all in the world.

Perhaps we are, in our smallness and insignificance, within the ranks of those few "just" ones thanks to whom the world will find forgiveness and will ultimately be saved. When the Judge of us all is about to raise his hand in punishment, we will intercede for you, together with the court of the saints. For we deserve holiness too; it is the life and existence of each one of us—if holiness means to do God's will, this we have been doing peacefully and joyfully for millions of years.

That day, you will hear us chirping, barking, mooing, tweeting, and meowing. Perhaps you will never understand the noise rising from stables, forests, branches of trees, and sides of hearths. You will never know that, if God grants you salvation, it will be because we interceded for you.

Our main virtue is perhaps to have no memory. That day, in fact, as I said, we will ask forgiveness for you because we will have forgotten all the beatings and the suffering that you inflicted upon us: the firing of the hunters in the bushes; the cruel traps that have seen us in agony for endless hours under the moon; the explosions battering the seabed and forcing our dead bodies to come to the surface effortlessly. All this we will have forgotten, and we will say instead: "Have mercy, Lord, for our masters." And we will do this because a man named Francis picked us up and kept us in the warmth of his hands, spoke simple words of love to us, and called us "brothers" and "sisters." And as long as he was alive, in us arose indeed that beautiful illusion: of being your brothers and sisters.

$\sim$

$\mathcal{I}$ am the nightingale, the most beautiful voice in nature. Pray, listen carefully, during full moon nights, to my joyful and desperate song among the branches. It is an intoxicating melody, yes, but listen more attentively; it is more. It is a mysterious liturgical litany. I am saying to my fellow animals: "In the name of St. Francis, let us intercede for them. . . ."

*If you love what he has made,*

*love still more him who has made it all.*

*If the creation is beautiful,*

*God who is reflected in it*

*is infinitely more beautiful.*

—ST. AUGUSTINE

# THE
## SWALLOWS

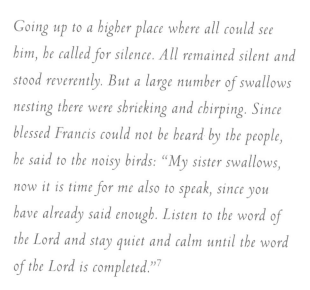

*Going up to a higher place where all could see him, he called for silence. All remained silent and stood reverently. But a large number of swallows nesting there were shrieking and chirping. Since blessed Francis could not be heard by the people, he said to the noisy birds: "My sister swallows, now it is time for me also to speak, since you have already said enough. Listen to the word of the Lord and stay quiet and calm until the word of the Lord is completed."[7]*

ND SO WE DID, SISTERS, REMEMBER? IT IS hard to explain how we managed to silently stifle our sweet and frantic shrieks. A frenzy thousands of centuries old takes a grip on us at dusk: a joyful spasm pierces us and throws us in the wide open air, in a thousand rapid twirls: in the gardens and around the towers and domes of the churches. We want people down below to notice us; we want them to respond and feel for our endless swarms some kind of rapturous envy.

So, we shriek while we are flying; and the sound inebriates us as it builds to a crescendo stronger than us, and places into our tiny chests a kind of blissful terror.

That is why it was almost a miracle, that evening in the Umbrian sky, that our hearing was able to perceive the voice of that little man—that tiny man who interrupted our noisemaking without shouting angrily, but rather by gently telling us to hush and quiet down because it was his turn to speak.

And when we were finally able to hear what he was saying, it was no longer such a great miracle for us to keep silent: because Francis's words arouse an enchanted peace in any creature listening to him—a thirst to continue hearing and relishing his words, even more beautiful than our wild carousel of flights and cries, which after all are part of our nature.

With that act of obedience and homage to the Creator of all beings, which indeed did not cost us any effort, we added that day to Francis—our brother and yours—a poignant but honorable remorse. For he, as Thomas of Celano writes in *The Treatise on the Miracles of Saint Francis*, "began to accuse himself of negligence because he had not preached to the birds before (since they so devoutly listened to the word of God). From that day on, he carefully exhorted birds and beasts and even insentient creatures to praise and love the Creator."[8]

# THE FALCON AT LA VERNA

*When blessed Francis, fleeing, as was his custom, from the sight of human company, came to stay in a certain hermitage place, a falcon nesting there bound itself to him in a great covenant of friendship. At nighttime with its calling and noise, it anticipated the hour when the saint would usually rise for the divine praises. The holy one of God was very grateful for this because the falcon's great concern for him shook him out of any sleeping-in. But when the saint was burdened more than usual by some illness, the falcon would spare him, and would not announce such early vigils. As if instructed by God, it would ring the bell of its voice with a light touch about dawn.[9]*

RUE, BIRDS OF ALL KINDS WERE ATTRACTED to Francis. But ours was a true friendship—and not only in words. I had the good fortune to build my nest at La Verna, where Francis was living in penance and got up each night to pray as mentioned in Celano's *Treatise on the Miracles of Saint Francis*. Thinking of the great effort it cost him to awaken, I would anticipate it with my loud cry, perhaps thinking my voice, though not beautiful, would assist such sacrifice.

He was very grateful, or at least he seemed to say so. But when I was made aware by some miraculous intuition that he was suffering from some ailment, I waited before waking him up, and until it seemed his breathing had returned to a regular pace and his face had regained a healthier color.

Thinking of the great effort it cost him to awaken,

I would anticipate it with my loud cry,

perhaps thinking my voice, though not beautiful,

would assist such sacrifice.

—THE FALCON

# THE
# WATER BIRD

*Heading to the hermitage of Greccio, blessed Francis was crossing the lake of Rieti in a small boat. A fisherman offered him a little water bird so he might rejoice in the Lord over it.*[10]

FRANCIS HAD NOT ONLY WORDS FOR US, but also softness and physical warmth, truly extraordinary, as if he felt what it meant to be a bird and knew that our primary need is a hiding place for refuge and protection.

So, on the lake of Rieti, when a fisherman caught me and offered me to Francis, and the saint gently urged me to fly away free, I could not imagine for myself a sweeter nest than his hands, and in those I settled. Nor did I want to leave my new abode. Francis had to implore me for a long time before I again felt the urge to fly away, with that freedom that our Creator intended for us. I reached into the vastness of the sky, finally, only after he had given me his blessing.

*In consideration of the primal origin*

*of all things, he would call all creatures,*

*however insignificant, by the names of*

*brother and sister since they come forth*

*with him from the one source.*

—ST. BONAVENTURE

# THE
# LARKS

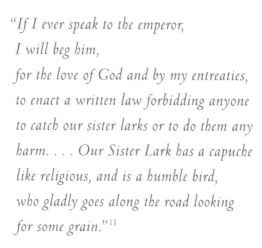

*"If I ever speak to the emperor,*
*I will beg him,*
*for the love of God and by my entreaties,*
*to enact a written law forbidding anyone*
*to catch our sister larks or to do them any*
*harm. . . . Our Sister Lark has a capuche*
*like religious, and is a humble bird,*
*who gladly goes along the road looking*
*for some grain."*[11]

HOMAS OF CELANO'S *THE TREATISE ON the Miracles of Saint Francis* speaks of us as well. It offers an account of that night when Francis passed from this world to Christ, when we gathered on the roof of the house "where they circled around noisily for a long while."[12] We sang with "tearful joy," as Thomas of Celano put it, "and joyful tears,"[13] almost as if we were mourning our own offspring and wanted to acknowledge in the same way the entry of this saint into God's eternal glory.

*That night when Francis passed*

*from this world to Christ,*

*when we gathered on the roof of the house*

*. . . We sang with "tearful joy."*

—THE LARKS

# THE
# PHEASANT

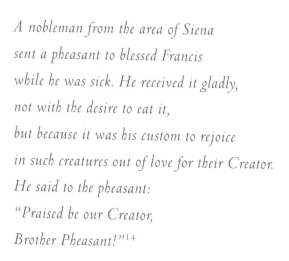

*A nobleman from the area of Siena*
*sent a pheasant to blessed Francis*
*while he was sick. He received it gladly,*
*not with the desire to eat it,*
*but because it was his custom to rejoice*
*in such creatures out of love for their Creator.*
*He said to the pheasant:*
*"Praised be our Creator,*
*Brother Pheasant!"*[14]

OU ARE RIGHT, WATER BIRD: WHAT WE SEEK
is a nest. And Francis—and with him also the
friendly brothers who shared his life—appeared to me as

the most benign place of refuge. If you read Celano's *The Treatise on the Miracles of Saint Francis*, it mentions me as well. When that noble man of Siena sent me as a gift to our blessed saint, so he could taste my delicious flesh, Francis greeted me as a brother and immediately said to his companions: "Let's make a test now to see if Brother Pheasant wants to remain with us, or if he'd rather return to his usual places, which are more fit for him."[15] Then a monk, obeying the saint's order, carried me in his hands and put me down in a vineyard. Immediately, with my rapid flight, I returned to the cell of the saint, who then ordered the monk to carry me further still. Once again, and with great speed, I returned to his cell and forced my way under the tunics of the monks in the doorway. So from that day I had the good fortune to be cared for and caressed by Francis, and my favorite hideaway was often the tunic of my sweet host and those of his brothers.

*The poverty and austerity*

*of Saint Francis were no mere*

*veneer of asceticism, but*

*something much more radical:*

*a refusal to turn reality*

*into an object simply to be used*

*and controlled.*

—POPE FRANCIS

# THE
# DOVES

*A young man one day caught many doves*
*and was carrying them off to sell.*
*Saint Francis met him and,*
*always having singular kindness*
*for meek animals,*
*looking at those doves with a look of pity,*
*said to the young man:*
*"O good young man,*
*I beg you to give them to me,*
*so that such innocent birds,*
*which are compared in Scripture to chaste,*
*humble, and faithful souls,*
*may not fall into the hands of cruel people*
*who will kill them."*

*The young man, inspired by God,*
*gave them all to Saint Francis,*
*and he taking them to his breast,*
*began to speak sweetly to them:*
*"O my sister doves, simple,*
*chaste, and innocent, why did you let yourselves*
*be caught? Now, you see, I want to rescue you*
*from death and make nests for you so that you*
*can bear fruit and multiply according to our*
*Creator's command."*[16]

# OTHER CREATURES

# THE
## FISH

*Another time he was travelling by boat on the same lake. When he arrived at the port, someone offered him a large fish that was still alive. Calling it "brother" in his usual way, he put it back next to the boat. The fish kept playing in the water in front of the saint, which made him very happy, and he praised Christ the Lord. The fish did not leave the spot until it was commanded by the saint.[17]*

ERE, IN OUR UNDERWATER WORLD, there is a perpetual, pristine, and unalterable happiness. The ease of movement with which we dart in every direction, in our fanciful schools, the liquid that surrounds us with its iridescent transparencies, make us creatures immersed in a constant, though expressionless and perhaps foolish, glee. We imitate joy, the "joy" that Francis lived and taught to people.

Neither perfect nor absolute is our joy. In fact, we easily move from an existence that is all joy to one of utter tragedy, when men with their hooks and nets snatch us from our undisturbed world. And then the earth's air is even worse than the hook that pierces our palate: it means for us death by suffocation; a short but terrible exile in an element that kills us.

I had a taste of that martyrdom, but, fortunately, it was short and had a happy ending. A fisherman of Lake Piediluco offered me to Francis, believing that such a gift would please him. I was left alone in the hands of the saint for just a few moments and, despite my lack of intelligence, I understood the words that he addressed to me, and from them I grasped a momentary respite to my despair, perhaps even some dim hope.

Francis told me what he had said to other fish, but in vain: do not let yourselves be caught. Therefore, he was on our side, even though his hands, which held me up with tender care, were of the same kind as those of the fisherman who had destined me to death. I ceased to thrash about, I remember now, in order to listen, to learn from the advice that he was giving me: "Now I will throw you back into your lake, sister, but be careful not to be caught again."

And since my gills were fluttering as I was struggling to breathe, Francis said nothing else; and then, after making a blessing sign on me, he threw me back in the water. In that moment, once I was able to dart around beneath the water foam, in my simple soul I immediately found again my usual happiness and joy. But there was also in me at that moment something else and different: the sense of having encountered, even there beyond my aquatic element in that world that for me means death, something beautiful and joyful; something I could call "love," if my simple nature were capable of grasping such a concept.

On the boat, looking down from one of the sides, Francis's face, with its scant beard, was smiling at me. It was a mischievous laugh of complicity, and I realized that he was telling me: "Sister fish, run away, and don't get caught again." It was his joy, so different from my own. Better still: it was his humor. But even this is a concept that I cannot grasp and understand. I only fleetingly understood it that morning, following the boat that was moving away, then diving down to the bottom of that small Umbrian lake.

*"Sister fish,*

*run away, and*

*don't get caught again."*

—ST. FRANCIS

# THE
# LITTLE RABBIT

*Once, while he was staying near the town of
Greccio, a certain brother brought him a live
rabbit caught in a trap. Seeing it, the most blessed
man was moved with tenderness. "Brother rabbit,"
he said, "come to me. Why did you let yourself
get caught?" As soon as the brother holding it let
go, the rabbit, without any prompting, took shelter
with the holy man, as in a most secure place,
resting in his bosom.*[18]

*Another time at Greccio a small live hare was
given to the man of God, who put it down on the
ground free to run away where it pleased. At the
call of the kind father, it leapt quickly into his lap.
He fondled it with the pious affection of his heart*

*and seemed to pity it like a mother. After warning it with gentle talk not to let itself be caught again, he let it go free. But as often as he placed it on the ground to run away, it always came back to the father's bosom, as if it perceived with some hidden sense of its heart the piety he had for it. Finally, at the father's command, the brothers carried it away to a safer place of solitude.*[19]

IF YOU ASK ME WHAT IS MY TRUE NATURE, the instinct that constantly guides my every emotion and movement, it is easy for me to answer— and I do so without shame: fear. For hundreds of thousands of years our destiny has been to flee, to find safety; we are in constant fear of everything, every little rustle in the bush, every blow of wind or movement of the water that may conceal some living being that could threaten our lives. Never, not even in sleep, or when we mate, are we free from this invisible trap of terror, this sense of danger looming over our tiny and fragile life.

Yet, it is all we have, and perhaps—precisely because we are always so threatened—we cherish it more than any other animal.

Even when we bear and take care of our offspring, there is no time for relaxation and idleness; actually, it is precisely then, in the pleasant warmth of the den, that the sense of a ruthless and fearsome threat obscures the joy of having given birth.

We rabbits fear every other animal, because we have very meager weapons to defend ourselves. Our fortune, or, if you will, the "grace" that the Creator bestowed upon us is nothing but our fast legs, this agility to jump and leap, always and everywhere driven by this blind and disproportionate fear.

But more than anything else, we fear humans. At times, a dog or a bird of prey, after breathless pursuits, gives up and decides to let us go, almost—if not out of mercy—as reward and recognition of our ability to outrun them. But not humans. They never give up their pride and the satisfaction in finally capturing us and bringing us to their homes hanging and bleeding from hooks, or stuffed in their game bags.

To achieve this, they have built boom sticks, which make useless the frantic zig-zag run we have always relied on to remain alive in the world.

That time, however—and I could not tell you how it happened—after being captured but then given an opening so I could escape, I did not run away. Actually, I stood near those men. And when Francis called me to him, I do not remember how, a force never felt before drove me to run toward him and even to jump on his chest.

Of course, as an eternal fugitive, my heart was still beating frantically—every moment we live is in our veins like a breathless escape. But his heart, which I could feel under his coarse sackcloth beating peacefully, gave me a sense of confidence and peace never felt before. No doubt, I would have never left the safety of that den (I was no longer thinking of the woods and my little family, which for sure was waiting for me) had he not spoken to me.

What did he say? My memory is confused; I only remember the feeling of a great kindness, like the sun when spring returns after the long cold, and from the sky it caresses us without having to fear some cruel ambush from its rays. But I still recall clearly his gentle admonition to never let myself be caught again, and to dedicate all my life to the enjoyment of the blessed happiness of being free. That same freedom, which I appreciated and knew so well, at that moment, I would have inexplicably exchanged for his company, for the safety and warmth of his hands, unarmed and full of caresses.

But Francis told me to go back to the woods. And almost reluctantly, and with no hurry, I obeyed. But I would meet my future with less fear, a secret sense of confidence even, because, as he put me back on the ground, he gave me his blessing.

*Saint Francis,*

*faithful to Scripture, invites us*

*to see nature as a magnificent book*

*in which God speaks to us and grants*

*us a glimpse of his infinite beauty*

*and goodness.*

—POPE FRANCIS

# JACOBA'S
# LAMB

*The mind of blessed Francis was filled with such great sweetness of divine love that, because he saw the marvelous work of the Creator in all things, he abounded in the greatest tenderness of piety toward all creatures. Yet, among those creatures, the ones he especially loved were those such as sheep, which he saw to be of a simpler and gentler nature, and whose names he had heard in the Scriptures, representing Christ because of their likeness to him.[20]*

*Once, in Rome, he had with him a little lamb out of reverence for the most gentle lamb of God. At his departure he left it in the care of a noble matron, the lady Jacoba of Settesoli.[21]*

WILL SPEAK FOR ALL OF US SHEEP,
who many times appear in Francis's life and
illustrations. Over the centuries, our innocence and our
querulous bleating have become the symbol—too often
conventional and sentimental—of this beloved saint.

Jacoba, Francis's devoted friend, was a witty and energetic
woman, far from any kind of sentimentality. She never
caressed me from the day when Francis—after redeeming
me at the animal market with some of the friars' meagre
savings, so I could escape the butcher's knife (my innocent
eyes and what seemed to him my likeness to the mystical
Lamb of Calvary moved him almost to tears)—handed
me to her. Thus, no sweet talk and caresses for me; just the
rugged shears she would shear me with twice a year, leaving
me hairless and trembling. She would do it with a kind of
impatience and greediness for my curly fleece. For with my
wool she would weave the warm clothes that, during the
cold winters, would keep her beloved teacher comfortable.

And this has been my privilege, by virtue of which at
least one of our species was able to repay Francis, in sincere

gratitude, for the kindness he always had for us sheep. No doubt, he honored us with generous and utmost esteem—perhaps because he saw us as the image of creaturely perfection and heavenly predilection—if to his closest companion, Brother Leo, he affably gave the nickname "little sheep of God."

The grace that I received from Francis that day—on the verge of being slain—I had the good fortune while I lived to repay, in some way, through the warmth of the soft cloth that came from my body. My mistress Jacoba and I, tied to Francis by various threads of obedience and love, ended up in a binding covenant of discreet complicity against Francis's too ascetic and negligent way of life—wearing rough clothes and eating irregularly whatever he could find.

So, I offered him the raw material for warm and comfortable clothes; and, in the end, I even learned to undergo Jacoba's scissors with joy. As you all know, she never forgot to make him her delicious pastries, with almond and honey, that the Romans call *mostaccioli*. And I was able to alert Jacoba, thanks to an understanding in the dark recesses of my mind—a sensitivity we animals have—so she could bring Francis her treats to enjoy one last time on his deathbed at San Damiano. I knew then that Jacoba would no longer need to remove the wool from my back—my offering to Francis on behalf of all my sisters of the flock.

*The grace that I received from Francis that day—on the verge of being slain—I had the good fortune while I lived to repay, in some way, through the warmth of the soft cloth that came from my body.*

—JACOBA'S LAMB

# THE
# CICADA

A cicada used to perch on a fig tree beside
St. Francis's cell at the Portiuncula and sing there,
inspiring the saint to praise God for its song,
because he could admire the glory of the Creator
in the most insignificant creature. Then one day
he called it, and when it hopped onto his hands as
if it had been taught by God, he told it, "Sing, my
sister cicada. Sing a song of praise to God your
Creator." Immediately the cicada started to chirp
and never stopped until the saint told it to go back
to its usual perch. There it remained for a whole
week and it came and went every day, singing at
his command.[22]

RANCIS'S HAND WAS SMALL AND smooth as that of a child. I can testify to it because a child once caught me from a branch. I had a tremendous scare in that closed fist—certain it would soon crush me. I do not remember how long my fear lasted; I only remember the child saying to his companions, "Now it will sing, you'll see," and then angrily to me: "Come on, sing, you stupid thing."

His companions bet that now that I was a prisoner, I would no longer sing, so the child shook me angrily and kept saying: "Come on, sing, or I'll crush you." And most certainly he would have done so, because I neither wanted to nor could obey him.

Suddenly, though, one of his companions hit his hand from behind. It opened, and I quickly took flight. For many days, I didn't have the heart to sing.

But it felt completely natural to glide onto the open hand of that man when he said, "Sister cicada, come here."

I love the great summer because I am its daughter. Under the heat of the sun, bark and leaves give off flavors and fragrances only I discern. It is wonderful to linger among them during torrid afternoons. From those hidden heights, I am the little sentinel of people's prolonged rests, their wild siestas, their frayed and lazy dreams. My song cradles their murkier fantasies and their sensual idleness as well; and yet, I am able to bestow a certain ironic innocence even on the noonday devil.

So I am happy during the short time of the summer season, which for me will not have a continuation, because I am too lazy to worry about winter and stock up on any provisions. My happiness is to stay where I am, invisible siren among the foliage, seducing people with that sole sentimental note of mine, which somehow is still a song. I am up here, away from their bodies and their treacherous hands ready to commit cruel acts.

But Francis—his hand had the scent of mulberry leaves and chestnut bark. His voice was so lovely, his tone so different from that child, when he told me to sing—to sing with my joy a praise of the Creator. After all, it is what my kind has been doing for millennia.

But it seemed to me the first time any sound came from my little body, hard-cased like a guitar, I felt like the first cicada ever in the world. Perhaps someone had told me he was a musician like myself, who had filled the hills of Umbria and France with the sound of guitar, his musical instrument very similar to mine.

Of course, I obeyed. I sang for a long time, as loud as I could. He said "joy" and I felt that in my fragile shell was contained all the joy of the earth and the heavens. It was a great delight—the deep awareness that every creature is made for joy and that joy can be expressed only in singing.

Then, after such a great effort, unusual for me, perhaps a sweet fatigue caught me. And when the saint commanded me to return "to my usual place," I promptly obeyed. But I was sure our separation was not forever, and that he would not forget me. And I taught the cicadas I have borne to wait for Francis's call, or that of another like him—if such a person can ever exist—before singing on an open hand.

*For Francis, these innocent beings, dragged into "exile" with Adam and Eve, help us to find, in our hearts and in the created world, the path back to innocence and happiness.*

—FR. NAZARENO FABBRETTI

# THE
## BEES

*While he was staying in a poor place
the holy man used to drink from a clay cup. After
his departure, with wonderful skill bees
had constructed little cells of their honeycomb
in it, wonderfully indicating
the divine contemplation
he drank in at that place.*[23]

I
T WAS OUR OWN QUEEN WHO GUIDED
our work in that clay cup. It was a common,
rugged mug, and we, common-minded workers. We did
not immediately understand the reason for building our
honeycomb in there, filling it with symmetrical cells.

We prefer to hang our honeycombs in a chestnut tree or
a linden tree where the branches meet, or inside a hollow

trunk. However, crammed into Francis's cup, we poor workers were overwhelmed with a sense of what to do. All of a sudden, we had the intelligence of our Queen— who knows all there is to know. We say intelligence, but perhaps this is not quite correct; we might better call it a sort of unswerving joy, of instinctive inventiveness. After all, even for humans—infinitely superior to us though you are—understanding and knowledge emanate from nothing other than flashes of that divine gift that is joy.

Joyful about what?, you may ask. Well, by condensing and placing our honey in that rugged mug, we felt we participated in the contemplation our brother Francis tasted, and in which he found relief when he was alive and dwelt among us here on earth. For surely his sips from the mug, to drink his "humble, precious, and chaste" water were moments not only of sustenance, but of innocent, intense, blissful contemplation—and of praise, from his wet lips and his refreshed tongue, to the One who created water, who created the mouth, thirst, and the wonder of uniting these things in a miracle that is not only of the senses but of the soul.

We bees make honey: from the flowers of the fields and trees, we know how to synthesize every pleasure and every sustenance for humans. Perhaps brother honey, with its varied and imaginative but also vigorous sweetness, is the masterpiece God has given to his creatures to produce.

And that great Bee that was Francis, after flying during his short life over all the flowers of creation, imitated us with an incomparable honey of words when before his death he sang the "Canticle of the Creatures." Yet, in that clay cup, he probably drank nothing but water. For that reason, our Queen wanted us to pay homage to him with our exquisite product, transforming that vessel that usually quenched his thirst with a comb full of savory sweetness that we alone are capable of producing.

And we bees can tell you that, among the thousands and thousands of flowers from which we usually go picking and choosing in order to obtain the most extraordinary nectar, no one has ever allowed us to enjoy a sweeter taste, a more sublime exaltation, than that humble cup where many times he had put his mouth. Never before have we felt more wonderfully the privilege, the mission, and the grace of being bees.

# CLARE'S CAT

*One time Lady Clare was not able to get out
of bed because of her illness. When she wanted a
certain towel to be brought to her and there was no
one to do so, a little cat in the monastery began to
pull and drag that towel to bring it to her as best
it could.*[24]

MAKE A LITTLE NOOK FOR ME AS WELL;
I want to be part of the Franciscan legend so as
to include along with myself all the animals of my species.
I am a cat, the "kitty" of the monastery of the Poor Clares.
I am part of their family; even my coat—like that of all the
most common cats—is a patchwork of white and black.

Cats, like dogs, are not prominent in the stories of Francis, perhaps because the relationships between domestic animals and people are not extraordinary or miraculous— anecdotes concerning the saint and his companions and pets are certainly numerous, but common and not worthy of being part of the saint's legend.

But I definitely did want to be part of Francis's legend. And, in the life of Saint Clare of Assisi—Francis's friend and one of his first followers, who in many ways was his mystical shadow—they do talk about me as well. My friendship with Clare (a female friendship, since that is who I was and who she was in the midst of all that male dominance) was indeed instrumental, albeit marginal, in the immense material gathered in support of her canonization.

We cats are not particularly intelligent, and above all we deserve the reputation of being unruly and stubborn before every instruction intended to bend us to the will of humans. But we do provide other comforts and other favors to them, and especially to their homes. We keep out mice and similar annoying tiny creatures; and then, with our happy purring, and our interminable winter naps cuddled by the fireplace, or our summer slumbers, under the sun embroidered by the vines in the openings of the yard, we cats represent the moment of bliss and gratitude— even though it is said that we are selfish and ungrateful. We become, as it were, the peaceful and living embodiment of the fact that people have created a warm home, a family where everything flows with the brisk serenity of the hours. We are the small and earthly "sacrament" of the house, of its existence around you, and of you in it.

As I just said, we are not particularly intelligent. So that time when Clare said she needed a towel and I realized that no one was able to help her, I had to first understand, with some unusual effort, what she intended; and then I had to force my indolent and independent nature a little bit to carry out the task. It was not easy for me to seize the towel by my teeth, dragging it as best as I could with its weight over the floor, and bringing it up to the saint who was lying ill in bed.

Clare, instead of thanking me right away, scolded me first because I had carried the towel like that, without lifting it up. So, I picked it up to the best of my abilities, that it not get dirty on the last stretch to her bed.

Thus, with that act of obedience and docility, and especially with that persistent effort to understand beyond the intellectual abilities that our Creator has bestowed upon me, turning into, albeit for just a short while, a humble servant instead of an ordinary cat, I have been recognized, after eight centuries, as a member of the chorus of animals that sing the glory of Francis.

*We [cats] become, as it were,*

*the peaceful and living embodiment of the*

*fact that people have created a warm home,*

*a family where everything flows with the*

*brisk serenity of the hours.*

—CLARE'S CAT

# THE
# WOLF

*Drawing close to him, Saint Francis made the
sign of the most holy cross on him and called him
to himself and said this: "Come here, Brother
Wolf. I command you on behalf of Christ that
you do no harm to me or to anyone." An amazing
thing to say! Immediately, when Saint Francis
had made the sign of the cross, the fearsome wolf
closed his mouth and stopped running; and once
the command was given, it came meekly as a
lamb, and threw itself to lie at the feet of Saint
Francis. And Saint Francis spoke to him thus: ". . .
Brother Wolf, I want to make peace between you
and these people, so that you do not offend them
anymore, and they may pardon you every past
offense, and so neither the people nor the dogs will*

*persecute you anymore." And after these words
were said, the wolf showed that he accepted what
Saint Francis said and wanted to observe it, by
movement of his body and tail and ears and by
bowing his head.*[25]

Y STORY IS TOO WELL KNOWN—
every child learns it at school in their early
years; and in the dreamy and misty learning of your little
children, I now stand in antithesis to another wolf: the one
in the Little Red Riding Hood fairy tale who is wicked and
without redemption, and who gobbles up the grandmother
and perhaps—if that tale had continued—would even kill
the child.

For your first and innocent wisdom (and hope), I
represent instead the proof and confirmation that evil is
not the ultimate reality of us creatures, but that it can be
converted to good; that there is also for us beasts, whose
appearance and conduct is most vile, a gesture, or a magic
word, or a potion capable of restoring the goodness in

us that made us all brothers and sisters at the dawn of the world. And, at the same time, I am the proof that gives the good and innocent ones relief from suffering more threats, and from having more doubts in God's benevolence toward them, or in God's almighty power capable of transforming ferocity into meekness, hatred into love.

At a sublime moment in history before me and the wolf in the fairy tale created by Charles Perrault, two other villains had already confirmed the possibility of being saved from evil and returned to goodness. I am thinking here about the two thieves on Calvary; the one on the right was able to transform blasphemy through supplication, and for this he heard in reply: "Truly I tell you, today you will be with me in Paradise" (Luke 23:43).

Even for him that fluid flickered, the exorcising word resounded, the key was found to open a heart believed to be made of stone and thorns.

What was the key for me? What words were able to spark the miracle that took place that day in Gubbio? As the tale goes, I was growling and running around with my jaws wide open; and even in front of Francis's reckless and trusting approach, I moved toward him with the same bloodthirsty hunger. What was it then?

If I were not an animal, and were able to analyze myself and be a historian of that moment so brief and so distant in time, I could answer that it was a cross and a voice. The cross that little man drew in the air a few feet from my red tongue thwarted my fury, and it caused a certain kind of dizziness. Following that wonderful sign came the voice of Francis—which had musical powers so intense you could understand the meaning well before he had finished his sentences. Most extraordinary of all, he immediately allowed me as well to "understand"—I who am a ravenous and fierce beast—the proposals and promises you can read in chapter 21 of the *Little Flowers of St. Francis*: first his reproaches for my misdemeanors; then peace with that small community of people I had terrorized; and finally the promise of food, protection, and companionship if I, "in the name of Jesus Christ," would cease to be a wolf and would become a new creature resembling nothing of me, or my father, or all my ancestors of the forest.

How I would like to be able to talk about the two years I lived with the people of Gubbio like any other animal, going "from door to door harming no one and not being harmed by anyone," and being fed by those families with such courtesy, without ever being attacked or barked at by any dog. And the tears of the people around me, that day when old age brought me to death.

But, instead, it would be better for you to engage in a more profound reflection; one that connects this miracle to the greatness of that little man, who, as St. Bonaventure put it, "had such remarkable gentleness and power that it subdued ferocious beasts, tamed the wild, trained the tame, and bent to his obedience the beasts that had rebelled against fallen humankind."[26]

Rebellious to humankind . . . why, how? Because humankind, well before us animals, wanted to rebel against God: Adam's first fall. And against the Creator, the wretched creatures continue to rebel; to scoff at the sign of the cross; to stifle any voice that says: "*I command you in the name of Jesus Christ*, come with me now, don't hesitate, so we can make this pact in the name of the Lord."[27]

The wolves that ravage your cities with terror, far more ruthlessly than I ever did in Gubbio, will never stop being beasts until you learn to speak to them with the loving music that extinguished the anger in my throat, until you raise your hand in that gesture that is not magical but divine. Until you yourselves go back to believing in that scaffold made of a post with a crossing bar, and in that man who was nailed on it and from which he was able to turn criminals into saints.

*Just as happens when we fall in love*

*with someone, whenever he would gaze*

*at the sun, the moon or the smallest of*

*animals, he burst into song, drawing*

*all other creatures into his praise.*

—POPE FRANCIS

# THE
# WORM

*He picks up little worms from the road so they will not be trampled underfoot.*[28]

I N WRITING WHAT YOU HAVE JUST READ above, Thomas of Celano risked the accusation of being a fraud and of inventing things. But Francis's biographer knew that leaving unreported this hardly credible and almost grotesque detail, he would have distorted and mutilated Francis's story just as if he would have silenced the resounding and glorious miracles. Yes, his fear of crushing us, of killing us—and others will say this fear, indeed a little peculiar, became an obsession for him: when the veil of blindness fell over his eyes, he would not dare to walk on any paths unless Brother Leo first assured him that he would not crush any of us under his sandals.

Yes, us—who go by the name of worms, and it is already surprising you have bothered to find a name for us in your language. A name, though, which resounds already of wretchedness, a synonym for abasement and disdain. We worms, or earthworms, are truly repulsive to look at—even more so when our slimy, tiny bodies twist between your fingers—and with the slobber we leave behind on pretty much everything we touch. For you, punishing us for our sordid existence under your feet while walking might be pleasing, if only that act did not evoke a shudder of revulsion in all of you. After all, even the soles of your shoes demand more respect.

But it is not so much for our ugliness and wretchedness that people abhor us. Rather, we are for them the *memento*, the reminder that one day in the mold of the grave we will triumph over them, gnawing at their flesh, which while they were alive they worshiped above all else, consuming them until the last bit.

So when you, who are neither Francis nor like him, crush us under your heels and burn down our burrows, you think you are acting on legitimate hatred while in reality you are deceiving yourselves with hope you can be spared the most humiliating form of decay after death.

Instead, one day, someone thought of us differently, as little brothers and sisters, and took great care so that his foot would not crush us. He bent down amid rocks and mud, taking us in his hand, and, after addressing us with a benign gaze, laid us down in a safe, grassy spot away from the beaten path.

So, in my opinion, he placed himself in possible comparison with that man named Jesus who said, "Truly I tell you, just as you did it to one of the least of these who are members of my family, you did it to me" (Matthew 25:40).

Well, am I not the least of those who share with you the same fate of existence—I am the most despicable, and certainly you cannot bother yourselves to call me "brother"? You cannot do it, and rightly so. Only a poet, who knew well how to share the absurd love of Christ, remembered us, poor filthy creatures, and wished to describe us as the shocking Glory with which our Savior deigned to clothe himself. Have you ever heard of Franz Werfel, who once wrote: But the Savior rose up and shouted—to the sky in a severe delirium . . . *"Father, you who are my Father—let me love these putrid creatures. . . . Can there be love where there is still disgust?"* [29]

# THE
## OX

*A man named Martin took his oxen far from home to find pasture. The leg of one ox was accidentally broken so badly that Martin could think of no remedy. He was concerned about getting the hide, but since he had no knife, he returned home and left the ox in the care of Saint Francis, lest wolves devour it before his return. Early next morning he returned to the ox with his skinning knife, but found the ox grazing peacefully; its broken leg could not be distinguished from the other.*[30]

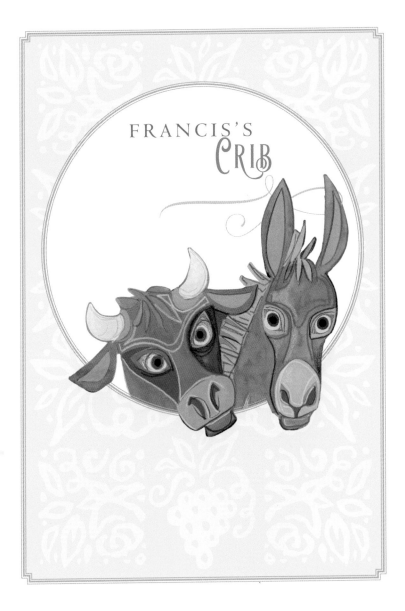

# FRANCIS'S CRIB

# CHRISTMAS EVE
## AT GRECCIO

"Also, out of reverence for the Son of God, whom
His Virgin Mother on that night laid in a
manger between an ox and ass, everyone
should have to give brother ox and brother ass
a generous portion of fodder on that night." . . .
For blessed Francis held the Nativity of the Lord
in greater reverence than any other of the Lord's
solemnities. . . . On that day he wanted every
Christian to rejoice in the Lord, and for love of
Him who gave Himself to us, wished everyone
to be cheerfully generous not only to the poor but
also to the animals and birds.[31]

HAT NIGHT OF CHRISTMAS EVE, 1223, when Francis, who had just spent long hours imagining the first crib and preparing it, fell asleep— exhausted after that remarkable effort—we remained awake throughout the earth.

On the hill of Greccio, Francis and his companions had bustled around with moss, twigs, and a few candles to shine under the starry night.

Appropriately, they chose an ox and ass and brought them alive within the walls of the cave. A few other animals were allowed to contemplate this new ritual—to watch Francis holding in his arms a mysterious child who soon disappeared—a few sheep and surely a goat, some farm dogs, rabbits, turkeys, the sorts of domestic or farm animals common in the Umbrian region who were not soundly asleep in their dens at that late hour.

We, then, we animals everywhere and of all kinds, we felt that night (or, to be more precise, the part after Francis had fallen asleep) that it was our duty to complete his work: that is, to endlessly enlarge that tiny corner of the world in front of which only a few shadows were visible, and make sure that Jesus's birth was extended all around the globe.

Thus, wherever we were, be it the jungle or the high mountains or the deep ocean, we came out of our dens; from the underwater caves where the fish cover up their eggs, and the inaccessible nests suspended at the top of the trees, and the underground tunnels dug by moles.

We came out without fear, as at a universal signal of truce, because we knew that each one of us would be completely absorbed by that moment on earth. The lion and the deer could stand side by side, and so could the frog and the stork, the turtle and the hawk, the snake and the mongoose; all of us giving up the hunt and the mating, the stocking up and the herding, in order to do something else and that only: attend to the crib Francis made.

An instinct stronger than our fear and our hunger called us that December 25th of 1223, at a celebration we felt was also our own—not only for humans and angels— our own at least since the man who created that unusual and ingenious scene persisted in calling each one of us his brother or sister, no matter how small and insignificant we were. And he never missed an opportunity to remind us to praise our Creator, as should every being. We felt that it was our feast also because Francis desired that "on such a solemn feast . . . every Christian . . . be cheerfully generous not only to the poor but also to the animals and birds."[32] And he made sure we were given "a generous portion of fodder" so that Christmas would remain, at least in our memory and expectation, a day for great food. Thus, we also could participate, with our primordial and never subsiding hunger, in that lavish feast that nowadays gladdens you humans immensely.

So for the remainder of that night, until the setting of the last star and the lightening of the sky, we stayed with our faces, our beaks, our horns, pointed toward that hill, in the ecstatic escape from our fear and our humiliation of being hunted, of being insignificant. Antelopes, monkeys, penguins, giraffes, ostriches, seals, chameleons, camels, beetles, flamingos, coyotes, frogs, jellyfish, armadillos—and other strange animals that Francis had never seen and did not even know existed: we all stayed awake in our very remote places, all around his blissful slumber—and his dreaming, perhaps, of the descent of new angels to finally bring to humans that much needed "good will" sung of on the slopes of Bethlehem twelve centuries before.

Meanwhile, the rest of humankind—of various races, creeds, and levels of cruelty—slept unaware, on the great sphere of the world. Those few milkers and gardeners of Greccio went to bed with more cheerful faces—after drinking a last goblet of wine and reciting an occasional prayer—without understanding much about what Francis had just given to all that night. But we animals, we stayed awake to look at that point in the west, that light perceptible only to us and our acute sense upon which our salvation is entrusted. We knew that each tiny space where we were crouched, though at the far ends of the planet, was still Francis's crib. And so, in silence, waiting for the dawn, we made Francis's crib more immense and more pleasing to the heart of God.

# NOTES

1   St. Augustine of Hippo, in Thomas Spidlik, *Drinking from the Hidden Fountain*, trans. Paul Drake (Kalamazoo, MI: Cistercian Publications, 1994), 270.

2   St. Bonaventure, in *The Minor Legend of Saint Francis*, in *Francis of Assisi: Early Documents* (hereafter FAED), vol. 2, 696–97.

3   Pope Francis, encyclical letter *Laudato Si'*, nos. 10-12. Copyright © 2015 by Libreria Editrice Vaticana; used by permission. http://w2.vatican.va/content/francesco/en/encyclicals /documents/papa-francesco_20150524_enciclica-laudato-si .html

4   Translator's Note: The original Italian edition was published in 1981.

5   *The Assisi Compilation, ch. 118,* in *FAED,* vol. 2, 227.

6   Charles Bonnet, *Palingénésie philosophique* (1767), 8.4.

7   *The Life of Saint Francis by Thomas of Celano*, 1.21; in *FAED*, vol. 1, 235.

8   *The Treatise on the Miracles of Saint Francis*, in *FAED*, vol. 2, 412.

9   *The Remembrance of the Desire of a Soul*, ch. 127; in *FAED*, vol. 2, 355–56.

10  *The Remembrance of the Desire of a Soul*, ch. 126; in *FAED*, vol. 2, 355.

11  *The Assisi Compilation*, ch. 14; in *FAED*, vol. 2, 129–30. A capuche is the hood or cowl typical of friars or monks from which the word *Capuchin* derives.

12  *The Treatise on the Miracles of Saint Francis*, ch. 4; in *FAED*, vol. 2, 415.

13  Ibid.

14  *The Remembrance of the Desire of a Soul*, ch. 129; in *FAED*, vol. 2, 356.

15  *The Treatise on the Miracles of Saint Francis*, ch. 4; in *FAED*, vol. 2, 413.

16  *The Little Flowers of Saint Francis*, ch. 22; in *FAED*, vol. 3, 604.

17  Ibid.

18  *The Life of Saint Francis*, ch. 21; in *FAED*, vol. 1, 235.

19  *The Major Legend of Saint Francis*, 8.8; in *FAED*, vol.2, 592.

20  *The Life of Saint Francis by Julian of Speyer*, ch. 9; in *FAED*, vol. 1, 399.

21  *The Major Legend of Saint Francis*, ch. 8; in *FAED*, vol. 2, 591.

22  *The Major Legend of Saint Francis*, ch. 8; in *FAED*, vol. 2, 695.

23  *The Treatise on the Miracles of Saint Francis*, ch. 4; in *FAED*, vol. 2, 414.

24  *The Acts of the Process of Canonization of Clare of Assisi*, in *Clare of Assisi: Early Documents* (New York: Franciscan Institute Publications, 1993), 167.

25  *The Little Flowers of Saint Francis*, ch. 21; in *FAED*, vol. 3, 602.

26  *The Major Legend of Saint Francis*, ch. 8; in *FAED*, vol. 2, 595.

27  *The Deeds of Blessed Francis and His Companions*, ch. 23; in *FAED*, vol. 3, 483.

28  *The Remembrance of the Desire of a Soul*, ch. 125; in *FAED*, vol. 2, 354.

29  Franz Werfel, "Jesus und der Äser-Weg," in *Neue Rundschau* 24 (1913), 1303.

30  *The Treatise on the Miracles of Saint Francis*, ch. 18; in *FAED*, vol. 2, 464.

31  *The Assisi Compilation*, ch. 14; in *FAED*, vol. 2, 129–30.

32  Ibid.

# ABOUT THE AUTHOR

LUIGI SANTUCCI (Milan, 1918–1999) was one of the most important Italian writers and poets of the second half of the twentieth century. He taught in high schools and worked at the Catholic University of Milan. In 1944, Santucci took refuge in Switzerland because of his opposition to the Italian fascist regime. Back in Milan, he was actively involved in the Italian Resistance, and was one of the co-founders of the underground newspaper *L'Uomo*, with poet David Maria Turoldo and others. Among his books translated into English are *Meeting Jesus—A New Way to Christ* (New York, Herder & Herder, 1971), one of the most original treatments of the life of Christ written in the twentieth century, and *Orfeo in Paradise* (New York, Knopf, 1969), winner in 1967 of Italy's prestigious Premio Campiello.

# ABOUT THE ILLUSTRATOR

MARTIN ERSPAMER, OSB, is a monk of St. Meinrad Archabbey in southern Indiana. He is a well-known liturgical artist and liturgical consultant. Erspamer works in a wide range of media, including pottery, stained glass, and wood, and is nationally known for his illustration of sacred themes.

For more information, please visit:
http://www.saintmeinrad.edu/stories/br-martin-erspamer/

# INDEX OF ILLUSTRATIONS

# ABOUT PARACLETE PRESS

## *Who We Are*

PARACLETE PRESS is a publisher of books, recordings, and DVDs on Christian spirituality. Our publishing represents a full expression of Christian belief and practice—from Catholic to Evangelical, from Protestant to Orthodox.

We are the publishing arm of the Community of Jesus, an ecumenical monastic community in the Benedictine tradition. As such, we are uniquely positioned in the marketplace without connection to a large corporation and with informal relationships to many branches and denominations of faith.

## *What We Are Doing*

PARACLETE PRESS BOOKS • Paraclete publishes books that show the richness and depth of what it means to be Christian. Although Benedictine spirituality is at the heart of who we are and all that we do, we publish books that reflect the Christian experience across many cultures, time periods, and houses of worship. We publish books that nourish the vibrant life of the church and its people.

We have several different series, including the best-selling Paraclete Essentials and Paraclete Giants series of classic texts in contemporary English; Voices from the Monastery—men and women monastics writing about living a spiritual life today; our award-winning Paraclete Poetry series as well as the Mount Tabor Books on the arts; best-selling gift books for children on the occasions of baptism and first communion; and the Active Prayer Series that brings creativity and liveliness to any life of prayer.

MOUNT TABOR BOOKS • Paraclete's newest series, Mount Tabor Books, focuses on the arts and literature as well as liturgical worship and spirituality, and was created in conjunction with the Mount Tabor Ecumenical Centre for Art and Spirituality in Barga, Italy.

PARACLETE RECORDINGS • From Gregorian chant to contemporary American choral works, our recordings celebrate the best of sacred choral music composed through the centuries that create a space for heaven and earth to intersect. Paraclete Recordings is the record label representing the internationally acclaimed choir Gloriæ Dei Cantores, praised for their "rapt and fathomless spiritual intensity" by *American Record Guide;* the Gloriæ Dei Cantores Schola, specializing in the study and performance of Gregorian chant; and the other instrumental artists of the Arts Empowering Life Foundation.

Paraclete Press is also privileged to be the exclusive North American distributor of the recordings of the Monastic Choir of St. Peter's Abbey in Solesmes, France, long considered to be a leading authority on Gregorian chant.

PARACLETE VIDEO • Our DVDs offer spiritual help, healing, and biblical guidance for a broad range of life issues including grief and loss, marriage, forgiveness, facing death, bullying, addictions, Alzheimer's, and spiritual formation.

Learn more about us at our website:
www.paracletepress.com
or phone us toll-free at 1.800.451.5006

SCAN
TO
READ
MORE

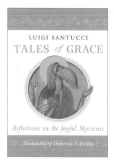
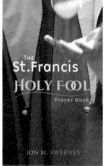